VIEWS IN THE HIGH PEAKS OF DERBYSHIRE

J C Bates
Advertiser Office, Buxton

THIS BOOK
was first published in 1884
by J C Bates
of the Advertiser Office, Buxton.

VIEWS IN THE HIGH PEAKS OF DERBYSHIRE

With an introduction by Mike Langham

The Silk Press
1999

PREFACE

The views in this book were commissioned by a Buxton printer and publisher, John Cumming Bates (1822-1899). He was the founder and proprietor of the *Buxton Advertiser* which, from its first edition in July 1852, became the principal newspaper of the town during the second half of the 19th century. As editor, he exerted significant influence, through his pen, on the growth of Buxton and he was an active force in the public life of the town and surrounding area.

By 1860 some very creative work was emanating from his press. He published a series of guide books which were illustrated by a few steel engravings. From these beginnings he went on to expand his portfolio of engravings to cover, not just Buxton, but the surrounding area of the High Peak of Derbyshire. It was quite usual to assemble such engravings into books of views for the tourists and these would be bound in various qualities determined by price.

J.C.Bates also published views of Buxton and its environs as prints, notable amongst which are the four panoramic views of Buxton taken from each side of the town. Inevitably the copies of these books which remain today are likely to be hard-backed, usually with embossed gilt decoration on the covers and therefore expensive to buy. Copies of the cheaper paper covered versions have quite often been broken up and the engravings framed as pictures.

This book faithfully reproduces Bates' engravings dating from the mid 1860s to about 1878, a period when the inland resort of Buxton and the surrounding Peak area saw a huge increase in visitors. It will, I am sure, be of immense value to all those interested in Derbyshire history. But I think that most people who turn the pages of this book will be fascinated by the detail and sharpness of these views which nineteenth century travellers would have taken home as a memento of their visit. We are fortunate that the Silk Press has chosen to make available this fascinating and rare series of views in a high quality but affordable format.

Mike Langham
Buxton, May 1999

LIST OF ILLUSTRATIONS

LEE WOOD HOTEL. CORBAR

Pub.d by John Cumming Bates, Advertiser Office.

THE PAVILION & GARDENS. ST JOHNS CHURCH. OLD HALL HOTEL. HOSPITAL. ST ANNS HOTEL.
NATURAL BATHS
GEORGE HOTEL

Panoramic View of Buxton.

Ent.d at Stationers Hall.

THE PALACE HOTEL   WYE HOUSE

CRESCENT.   ADVERTISER OFFICE.   HOT BATHS.   QUADRANT   N. W & MIDLAND RY STATIONS.

Engd. by Newman & Co. 48 Watling St. London.

GROVE HOTEL.   ROYAL HOTEL.

"The elegant equipages moving to and fro in the crescent added a grace and interest to the scene - altogether forming such a picture of life and energy as could hardly be expected to be found amid the barren heaths of the Peak."

William Adam 'Gem of the Peak' 1851

The St. Ann's Crescent, Old Hall & Palace Hotels, Buxton

"The Old Hall Hotel is the only building in Buxton (except the Old Church) which is more than two hundred years old. The present commodious edifice was erected in 1670 by the third Earl of Devonshire, on the site of a former one, which was described in 1572 as 'a fine mansion - a very goodly house, four square, four storeys high. .... It is a comfortable and fashionable hostelry, its central situation adding to its desirability as a temporary home."

Ward Lock's Illustrated Guide

Eng by Newman & Co 48 Watling St London

The Old Hall. Buxton

Where Mary Queen of Scots resided.

"The Hot Baths, in which the water is raised to a temperature ten or twelve degrees higher than the natural heat of the springs, are located in an elegant glass and iron structure at the eastern end of the Crescent, with the colonnade of which it is connected by a glass-roofed arcade; this protects invalids from the exposure to the weather. The accommodation comprises eighteen private baths."

Ward Lock's Illustrated Guide

Pub. by J.C. Bates, Buxton.

Eng. by Newman & Co. 48 Watling St. London

The Hot Baths, Buxton.

"The Terrace Walks .... have been provided with broad, well gravelled and dry footpaths; by these the extent of the walks in the immediate neighbourhood of the town may be fairly said to have doubled within the last few years. .... and are kept in order at the sole cost of the Duke of Devonshire."

Ward Lock's Illustrated Guide

The Terrace & Hall Bank, Buxton.

"The Congregational Church, Hardwick Street - a handsome Gothic structure."

Ward Lock's Illustrated Guide

Congregational Church. Buxton.

"The Devonshire Hospital was opened for the reception of the patients of charity in the year 1859. It is the successful result of the conversion of a very extensive range of buildings, erected and used as stables since the commencement of the present century, and situated on a commanding eminence, presenting views of the town and valley of Buxton ...."

Ward Lock's Illustrated Guide

The Devonshire Hospital, Buxton.

Cavendish Villas, erected for Mr Barnard, wine and spirit merchant was the first property to be built on Cavendish terrace in 1861 and the area soon became one of the most fashionable parts of the town.

Cavendish Villas, Buxton.

THORNCLIFFE.   MALVERN HOUSE   WESLEYAN CHAPEL. PROSPEC

CAVENDISH VILLAS.   GROSVENOR VILLAS.   HOLLY BANK.   MILTON HOUSE.   CAVENDISH HOUSE.

Panoramic View of Cavendish Terrace, Buxton.

Ent'd at Stationers Hall.

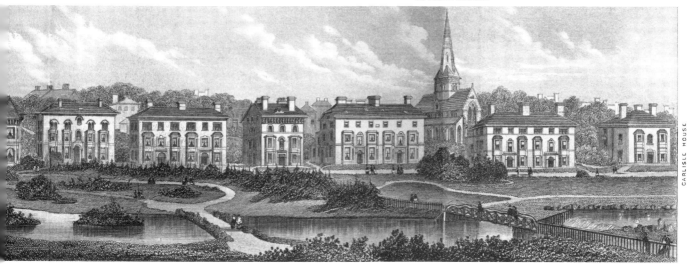

ST JAMES' CHURCH.

CARLISLE HOUSE

HOUSE   STANLEY VILLAS.   LAKE VILLAS.   DALTON HOUSE   CAMBRIDGE VILLAS.   WESTMINSTER HOUSE   ETON HOUSE.

Engᵈ by Newman & 48 Watling St London.

"....the Conveyance of twelve acres of land by the Duke of Devonshire .... was made without charge, on condition that the ground be enclosed and embellished by landscape gardening, and that a suitable building be provided in which the band might perform in unpropitious weather ...."

Ward Lock's Illustrated Guide

Pub. by T. Bates Advertiser Office, Buxton.

Eng. by Newman & Co. 48 Watling St London.

The Pavilion, Buxton Gardens

"........a large pavilion was erected, composed of glass, iron and wood, and including central hall, corridors and terminal conservatories, 120 yards in length ...... with a terrace promenade in front, of the same length and width."

Ward Lock's Illustrated Guide

Pub. by J. C. Bates, Adv.^r Office, Buxton.

Eng.d by Newman & Co. Watling St London.

Interior of Pavilion, Buxton Gardens

"..... it has a southern aspect and there are grassy slopes and walks down to the river Wye, which is crossed by a handsome bridge, ornamented with flower vases and gas lamps."

Ward Lock's Illustrated Guide

Cascade & Bridge in the Buxton Gardens

"The bridge leads to a central bandstand, from which another bridge and broad walks lead to ornamental waters, artistic rock works and an extensive croquet lawn."

Ward Lock's Illustrated Guide

Pub. by A.A. Bailie Adv. Office, Buxton.

Eng. by Newman, 48 Watling St. London.

Alpine Garden & Croquet Lawn in the Buxton Gardens.

"...... a succession of floral beauty at different seasons of the year has been secured by extensive forcing pits. The charge for admission is fourpence (or sixpence after 5pm), a sum which is decreased when a ticket is taken for a week, month or year."

Ward Lock's Illustrated Guide

Pub by I.C. Bates, Advertiser Office, Buxton.

Eng by Newman, & C. 48. Watling, St. London.

View in Buxton Gardens.

"In the year 1880 a further addition was made to the already extensive grounds, by purchasing or renting from the Duke of Devonshire a triangular piece of land, seven acres in extent, including a lake which is used for boating, This has proved a great attraction .... "

Ward Lock's Illustrated Guide

The Lake in the Buxton Gardens.

"The Gardens are beautifully laid out, are kept in admirable order, and at night are illuminated by electricity. In front of the Pavilion a wide terrace-promenade extends for its whole length, and from it walks diverge to every nook and corner of the grounds, which are more than 20 acres in extent. They have a southern aspect, and the infant Wye, 'which has just emerged from its limestone cradle, is tortured and twisted, and made to meander all about them, and to fall over several artificial cascades, before it is allowed to enter the tunnel which carries it beneath the adjoining Crescent and other parts of the town'."

Ward Lock's Illustrated Guide

The Gardens, Buxton.

"A terrace-walk called Cavendish Terrace, of considerable breadth and with the advantage of being almost level, extends in the direction of Poole's Cavern ...... it is one third of a mile in length, is dry and well made and affords splendid views of the gardens, plantations, park, Corbar Wood, Burbage and Burbage Edge."

Ward Lock's Illustrated Guide

Pub. by J.C. Bates, Buxton.

Eng. by Newman & Co 48 Watling st London.

Cavendish Terrace, Buxton

BEET WOOD   LONG HILL   ROBIN HOOD TOR NITHEN END COOMBS MOSS CORBAR CUCKOO TORS

CRINWOOD

Pub.d by John Cumming Bates, Advertiser Office.

Buxton from Solomon's Temple,
(looking East.)

EDGE   DOVE HOLES   FAIR.FIELD   MAM . TOR   TIDESWELL MOOR
               LIME WORKS

DUKE'S DRIVE.

SHERBROOK
QUARRY

Eng.d by Newman. & Co. 48.Watling S.t London.

"Open to the public, the Serpentine walks are beyond the enclosed grounds of the Buxton Improvements Company; they are very picturesque wooded walks by the banks of the river ...."

Ward Lock's Illustrated Guide

Rustic Bridge, Serpentine Waters, Buxton.

"The stream is made highly interesting by being deepened in places to give a greater expanse of water, and banked up in others to form miniature cascades.
At suitable and convenient distances, seats, alcoves or rustic summer houses are made for the comfort of the invalid."

William Adam 'Gem of the Peak' 1851

Pub. by J. & J. C. Bates, Buxton.

Eng. by Newman & Co. 48 Watling St. London.

Rustic Bridge, Serpentine Walks, Buxton.

"The walks were thronged with the gay and the lighthearted of all ages in the higher and middle walks of life, brought together from different parts of the three kingdoms and the great world. The rapid movements of the young and the healthy contrasted strangely with the slow and painful movements of a few individuals scattered amongst the throng, who, however were generally found to prefer the low instead of the high ground ...."

William Adam 'Gem of the Peak' 1851

The Gardens, Buxton.

"The church of St Peter's was built in 1838, on the site of an older one. .... it is a plain and unpretending structure, with a square pinnacled tower, containing six bells. ....there is in the churchyard a fragment of a sun dial."

Ward Lock's Illustrated Guide

Pub. by J & J.C. Bates.

Eng. by Newman & Co. 48, Watling St. London.

Fairfield Church, Buxton.

"New arrivals at Milton House, Cavendish Terrace (Mrs Rogers and Mrs Darcy): Mr. Mrs and Miss Adairs. Whalley Range, Manchester; Miss Grafton, Manchester; Miss Thorpe, Southport: Mrs Coulthard, The Grove, Popcastle; Mr and Mrs Ashton, Whitefriars, Penwortham; Mrs and Miss Peel, Swinton Park, near Manchester."

"Buxton Advertiser and List of Visitors", 6 May 1876

Milton House, Broad Walk, Buxton.

MALVERN HOUSE HYDROPATHIC ESTABLISHMENT, BUXTON.

Sheltered from the north and east and within four minute's walk of the

Baths and Gardens ....

Entirely New Bath Rooms with all Modern Improvements.....

For Particulars, apply to the Manager

Contemporary advertisement 1882

Pub.by J. C. Bates, Advertiser Office, Buxton.

Eng.d by Newman & Co. 48 Watling St. London.

Malvern House, Hydropathic Establishment, Buxton.

"Clarendon House is pleasantly situated within five minute's walk of the Baths, the Public Gardens and the station. It faces south-west and the temperature is so regulated as to make the house suitable for winter as well as summer residence."

Ward Lock's Illustrated Guide

Clarendon House. Devonshire Park. Buxton.

Edward Webster, Proprietor.

"The Old Market Square in Higher Buxton is adorned with trees and has in the centre the restored Market Cross of the town."

Ward Lock's Illustrated Guide

Pub by J. C. Bates, Buxton.

Eng by Newman & Co 48 Watling St. London.

Market Place, Buxton.

"The Lee Wood, in Devonshire Park ...... large and handsome.... a comfortable and well-conducted establishment ...."

Ward Lock's Illustrated Guide

Lee Wood Hotel

Brian Bates, Proprietor

"*The more energetic pedestrian should ascend beyond the highest limits of the Corbar Wood Walks, pass through an upper plantation, and reach the summit of Corbar Hill, which commands an extensive view of Buxton and Fairfield.*"

Ward Lock's Illustrated Guide

Pub.d by Bate Brothers, Buxton.

Eng.d by Newman & Co. 48 Watling St. London.

Buxton from Corber.

PRIEST CLIFF   CHELMORTON LOW   STADEN LOW   FOX LOW AND HARPER HILL LIME W

FAIRFIELD

Pubd by John Cumming Bates, Advertiser Office.

Buxton from Corbar Crag.
(looking South.)

GRINLOW,
OR SOLOMON'S TEMPLE

LEEK ROAD,
BUXTON LIMEWORKS.   AXE EDGE

MACCLESFIELD   HIGH PEAK
ROAD   RAILWAY

Engᵈ by Newman & Cᵒ 48 Watling Sᵗ London.

"The cavern is one of the chief attractions of the neighbourhood ....
Its entrance is very narrow, and on its left side a number of human and other bones were discovered, in the course of widening and levelling the sides and bottom of the opening, which show that its existence was known long before the appearance of the Romans in the island."

Ward Lock's Illustrated Guide

Pub. by J.C. Bates, Buxton.

Eng. by Newman & Co. 48, Watling St. London.

Entrance to Poole Cavern, Buxton.

"The overhanging masses of rock, covered with stalactites, have a bold and imposing appearance.. The Cavern here is lofty and when properly lit has a most magnificent effect. .... the cavern, with its rich and curious incrustations, is well worth a visit, and especially from the interest thrown around it by the visit of Mary, Queen of Scots."

William Adam 'Gem of the Peak' 1851

Pub by J.C.Bates, Buxton.

Eng by Newman & C.º 48. Walling St London.

Interior of Poole Cavern, Buxton.

"A great portion of the summit of Grin Low is covered with dross and slag, the refuse of the neighbouring limekilns. Many of these mine hillocks have been excavated, and were formerly the habitation of human beings - - generally a small aperture in the side answered the purpose of a window, and an opening through the roof served to carry off the smoke from the interior. Through the exertions of the late Mr Wilmot, the agent of the Duke of Devonshire, these wretched hovels have been destroyed, and in their stead a number of neat and comfortable dwellings have been erected at Burbage..."

J Croston "On Foot in the Peak" 1876

Pub.d by Bates Brothers, Buxton.

Eng.d by Newman & Cº 48, Watling St. London.

Miners Cottage, near Buxton.

"A pretty little church of Norman architecture, Christ Church was erected in 1861.
Its tower contains an illuminated clock and a peal of five sweet-toned bells, and most
of the windows have been filled with stained glass."

Ward Lock's Illustrated Guide

Pub. by John Cumming Bates, Advertiser Office.

Eng. by Newman & Co. 48, Watling St. London.

Christ Church, Burbage.
(near Buxton)

"At the entrance to Sherwood Dell is a lofty rock, rejoicing in the title of Lover's Leap. There are various accounts of the origin of this name, Jewitt ascribes it to the fact that in the year 1876 a love-sick maiden named Hannah Baddeley threw herself from the summit .... her fall was broken by a tree and her life was thus saved; but she remained a cripple for the remainder of her days. Another legend traces the name to a desperate, but successful, leap of two runaway lovers, riding one horse, who thus evaded the pursuit of the lady's parents and were 'married and lived happily ever after', of course."

Ward Lock's Illustrated Guide

Waterfall at Lovers Leap, Buxton.

"...... on reaching the north eastern corner of the belt of plantation the track may be left and the eastern edge followed for quarter of a mile or less, when the top of the lofty and abrupt rocks which bound the north side of Ashwood Dale will be reached, and a bird's eye view obtained of the road, the river and the railway, with all their very picturesque and beautiful surroundings."

Ward Lock's Illustrated Guide

Ashwood Dale, Buxton.

"We come to the junction of the Buxton and Manchester lines (at Blackwell Mill). Here we turn left to Buxton, and pursue our way by a course full of interest and beauty. The lofty crags are covered with masses of ivy, and on every ledge, round every base, are tangled woods of ash, and oak, and birch; and every spot is the home of rooks and daws and starlings innumerable. Near Topley Pike, which we see on the left, we enter a tunnel. It is the back of Pig Tor. a "savage looking headland"; and on emerging from the gloom. we enter Ashwell Dale and immediately pass the ivy shrouded toll-house in the valley below, where the line crosses the road by a lofty viaduct."

F S Williams "The Midland Railway" 1877

Pig Tor Bridge & Tunnel.
(near Buxton,

"We observed to our right, and but a short distance from us, the towering hill of Priest Cliff, the giant base of which skirts the greater part of Blackwall Dale on the south side and where quartz crystals, or what are termed 'Derbyshire diamonds' may be obtained among the loose matter on the side of the Cliff."

William Adam 'Gem of the Peak' 1851

Pub by J C Bates, Buxton.

Eng by Newman & Co 48, Watling St. London.

Blackwell Dale, near Buxton.

"We proceeded but a little way before we found ourselves surrounded on all sides by lofty overhanging crags, in some places quite inaccessible; and before we had proceeded three-quarters of a mile, we were stopped altogether by the character of the pass. Hitherto the rocks were confined to the top of the steep acclivities, but here was presented one awful rocky chasm from the bed of the stream to the top of the deep dale, and so narrow that the river passes beneath their shelving masses, and, darkened by their shadow, its sparkling waters are converted into a dark and gloomy pool, or yawning gulf, fearful enough to look upon. The whole space from hence, till the river emerges from the base of Chee Tor, is of a similar character. .... And surely if there is a spot where the heart quails beneath the majesty of God, as exhibited in his works, it will do so here, in witnessing the wild scenery around and beneath the Tor There is decidedly nothing like it in Derbyshire."

William Adam 'Gem of the Peak' 1851

Pub. by J C Bates Buxton.

Eng. by Newman & Co 48 Watling St London.

Chee Dale near Buxton.

"This is one of the most remarkable Tors in Derbyshire .... which assumes the form of a magnificent curve, like a mighty Crescent .... the top is deeply fissured and covered with light and elegant foliage .... the opposite Rock takes a splendid sweep, answerable to the curve of the Tor, but assumes a different character, being divided into bands or ledges, and overhanging the chasm in places some yards, which, with the pendant foliage, looks like a spacious alcove, fit for giants to repose in."

William Adam 'Gem of the Peak' 1851

Pub. by J. C. Bates, Buxton.

Eng by Bowman & Co. 8 & 9 Whitby, London.

Chee Tor, near Buxton.

"....... a series of crags rising one above another, terminated by the gigantic overhanging rock of Raven's Tor, bound the view; the intermediate spaces filled up by bold eminences, covered with verdure, and the rippling and sparkling river flowing between."

William Adam 'Gem of the Peak' 1851

Pubd by J. C. Bates, Buxton.

Engd by Newman & Co 48 Watling St London.

Miller's Dale near Buxton.

"At Litton Mill the Dale becomes impassable for carriages and we had therefore to take up the remarkably steep hill to get to Cressbrook. About three parts up this lofty eminence we had a most magnificent view of an immense district to the south east and west."

William Adam 'Gem of the Peak' 1851

Pub by J.C. Bates, Buxton.

Eng. by Newman & Co 48 Watling St London.

Cressbrook Dale & Mill near Buxton.

"The dale forms part of the valley of the Wye. On the sides of the river are a few white cottages which form the hamlet of Miller's Dale ."

Ward Lock's Illustrated Guide

Pub.d by T.C.Bates, Buxton.

Eng.d by Newman & Co. 48 Watling St London.

Miller's Dale near Buxton.

(Looking towards Cressbrook.)

"Chatsworth House is remarkable from its great size, its adaptation to the scenery which surrounds it, its upland background of dark woods, which shelter an arboretum of much botanical value, its gigantic fountains and waterworks, its great rockworks, its conservatories, orchid-houses, gardens, and pleasure-grounds, its Italian facades, its princely suites of rooms, its choicely filled sculpture gallery, its paintings and drawings by great masters, ancient and modern, and its extensive and valuable library .... The surrounding grounds and gardens are on a magnificent scale, and for these even the genius of Paxton could do no more as to taste and design."

Ward Lock's Illustrated Guide

Sold by Bates Brothers, Buxton.

Eng. by Newman & Co. 48. Watling St London.

Chatsworth, Derbyshire

"The bold ridge on which Haddon stood, covered with thick woods, formed its eastern boundary; and to the north might be seen Longstone Edge, the great Finn, and the lofty eminences near to Buxton; to the south, appeared the beautiful wooded knolls of Stanton and Darley.

To enjoy such a splendid prospect to its utmost verge we ascended the rude steps of the Watch Tower. The two dear friends who accompanied me, and who had never visited this part of the Peak till now, were so affected with the richness, extent, and glory of the scene, that they remained for a time perfectly silent, wrapped up in the enjoyment of those delicious emotions which are the result of surprise, delight, and wonder, and which were enhanced in a tenfold degree by the immediate transition from Haddon's deserted halls, to a scene of such interest, animation, and beauty."

William Adam 'Gem of the Peak' 1851

Pub. by C. Bâtes, Crescent, Buxton.   Eng.^d by Newman & C.° 48 Watling St London.

Haddon Hall.
(from the Garden.)

"Matlock has a more modern history than Buxton, very little being known of it before the year 1698, when the curative qualities of its waters first began to attract attention. There is no doubt that the spot was occupied by the Romans, and occasionally antiquarian research brings to light evidences of the former value of the lead mines in the neighbourhood. But its present popularity may be said to date from the construction of the railway, which annually enables thousands of tourists to visit the place. It is beyond all doubt a very beautiful place, and its attractions fully justify the encomium of Lord Byron, when he declared, "I can assure you there are things in Derbyshire as noble as in Greece or in Switzerland.""

Ward Lock's Illustrated Guide

Sold by Bates Brothers, Buxton.

Eng. by Newman & Co. 48. Watling St London.

Matlock, Derbyshire.

"The view from the top is not commanding, but deeply interesting, from being clothed to the very edge with fine green fields and good pasture ground, and a party from these fields may safely approach to the verge of a precipice, which makes the stoutest heart tremble in looking down it, and the clearest head giddy."

William Adam 'Gem of the Peak' 1851

The High Tor, Matlock.

"The village of Castleton, which derives its name from this ancient stronghold, is situated near the bottom of the steep eminence at whose feet the famous cavern discloses itself; and whose summit is occupied by the ruins of the ancient castle of the Peverils. Near the entrance of the village a bridge has been thrown across the stream which issues from the cavern. The buildings are chiefly of stone. The support of the inhabitants is derived from the mining business, and from the expenditure of those who are induced to visit the remarkable places in the neighbourhood. A ditch and vallum formerly extended in a semi-circular course round the village, from the mountain on which the castle stands, and may yet be traced in particular directions."

William Adam 'Gem of the Peak' 1851

Pub. by Bate's Brothers, Buxton.

Eng. by Newman & Co. 48, Watling St. London.

Castleton.

"The entire length of this wonderful cavern is seven hundred and fifty yards, and its depth from the surface of the mountain, above two hundred and seven. It is wholly formed in the limestone strata, which are full of marine exuviœ, and occasionally display an intermixture of chert. From different parts of the cavern some communications open with other fissures; but none of these equal it either in extent or grandeur. Through one of these, a very large fissure to the left, immense quantities of fragments of stone and debris are thrown out, perhaps from the Speedwell Mine level and the basin at Perry-Foot, as already noticed, which may empty their waters into this cavern. In extremely wet weather the interior cannot be visited, as the water fills up a great portion of the cavern, and rises to a considerable height even near the entrance: at other times the access is not very difficult."

William Adam 'Gem of the Peak' 1851

Eng by Newman & Co 48 Watling St London.

Peak Cavern & Peveril Castle, Castleton.

"This wild ravine is bound on each side by perpendicular rocks of amazing height; yet it is not wholely devoid of beauty; numbers of rare and elegant plants picturesquely adorn the steeply sides of this, in other respects, deep, lonely and dreary pass ....."

'Murder of Allan & Clara, (two lovers), in the Winnats.'
William Wood 1843

Pub. by Paine Brothers, Buxton.

Eng by Newman & C.º 48, Watling St London.

Shining Tor. Winnats. Castleton.

"The approach is grand and truly imposing, the massive ramparts rising to a prodigious height on each side. The right hand part of the face of the rock on the left, is fringed with trees and shrubs. The hoarse scream of the jackdaws adds to the wild and savage character of the place, and the lofty and apparently critical position of the Castle perched on the top, and immediately over the arch on the left, considerably heightens the feeling. Approaching the mouth, the shrill cry of the cord-winders, and the busy hum of their numerous twisting-wheels, strike the ear with a hollow and unnatural sound, as if the interior were peopled by imaginary beings.
.... a vast canopy of unpillared rock, assuming the appearance of a depressed arch, forms the mouth of this stupendous excavation. This arch is regular in its structure, and extends, in width, one hundred and twenty feet; in height, forty-two; and in receding depth, upwards of one hundred. Proceeding about thirty yards, the roof becomes lower, and a gentle descent conducts, by a detached rock, to the interior entrance of this tremendous cavern. Here the blaze of day, which has been gradually softening, wholly disappears, and all further passage must be explored by torchlight."

William Adam 'Gem of the Peak' 1851

Entrance to Peak Cavern
Derbyshire.

"The new house, erected but a few years ago, is a castellated structure, chiefly in the Elizabethan style. This fine mansion, and the lovely scenery around, seem in perfect unison with each other, and when beheld from the road leading along the side of Bunster hill, near the gate, the view is peculiarly rich and beautiful. The grounds are kept in admirable order, and the cottages which we passed are remarkably neat and clean."

William Adam 'Gem of the Peak' 1851

Pub. by J. & J. C. Bates Winster Place, Buxton

Eng. by Newman & Co 48, Watling St London

Ilam Hall.

The Seat of Jesse Watts Russell, Esqre

"Dovedale Church — The foliage around the base of these rocks, and from amongst their clefts, is most luxuriant, adding grace and beauty to their majestic forms. The scenery here is so bold, beautiful, and impressive, that few lovers of the pencil could leave the Dale without, if time permitted, transferring its shadowy resemblance to their sketch-books.

On reaching the meadow, where the Dale expands considerably, we find on the right a number of bold rocks ridging the mountain side, jagged and broken for the most part, and clothed fantastically and beautifully with ivy and creeping plants, the clefts between them filled with the hazel and dwarf ash, and an abundance of indigenous plants, which give a beauty and deep interest to this colossal group, called, 'Tissington Spires,' or the 'Twelve Apostles.'"

William Adam 'Gem of the Peak' 1851

Dove Dale Church & Tissington Spires.

Eng. & Pub. by Newman & Co. 48 Watling St London.

"Here we were presented with the first view of the beautiful scenery of Dovedale. As we stood on the margin of the lovely stream, Thorpe Cloud was exhibited in its most imposing aspect — lofty and remarkably steep, and apparently terminating in a cone or circular point, forming, with Bunster Hill, opposite, the stupendous portals of the Dale. Here we beheld the beauty of the stream, which is much enhanced by a series of rough stony embankments, dividing it into numberless cascades of surpassing loveliness. The verdant meadow fringes its margin, and spreads on either hand till it reaches the steep and sterile mountain side."

William Adam 'Gem of the Peak' 1851

Eng. & Pub. by Newman & Co. 48 Watling St. London.

Entrance to Dove Dale from Thorpe.

"The surrounding country is rich in Druidical remains; and the place derives its name from the water-swallows in the neighbourhood, among the most remarkable in Derbyshire. A water-swallow hole is caused by the disappearance of a stream of water, which descends into an underground natural channel, and emerges to the surface at a distance, in some cases of several miles. In many instances, when the streams are full, the swallow is unable to receive the whole of the water, and the diminished flow continues its course along the surface; whereas, in dry weather, the swallow receives the entire stream.

Barmoor Clough, about a mile and a half from Dove Holes, is the site of one of the most remarkable of the intermitting springs of this district."

Ward Lock's Illustrated Guide

Eng. & Pub. by Newmans C. 48. Watling S. London.

The Dove Holes, Dove Dale.

"......... the view from hence will amply repay the time and trouble. To the right, the Dale assumes its wildest character; becoming a gloomy and cheerless glen, shut in by huge perpendicular rocks, overhung with brushwood — the river fretting and foaming over the rocky bed, and struggling to free itself from the dark recess. The Cave is not spacious, but remarkably uneven and fretted, the roof circular, and giving full effect to the voice, which we failed not to try by attempting a chorus in the Messiah. The effect was magnificent and thrilling — surrounded with such objects as exhibit in legible characters the majesty of God.

After resting awhile, under the full influence of those feelings elicited by our employment, we next visited the adjoining Cave, called Renard's Kitchen, and then made our way carefully down the fearful steep to explore the remaining part towards the northern entrance. It is said this Cave received its name from a robber called Renard, who used to frequent it. Parties frequently make this their resting point, take luncheon, and sometimes boil the kettle for tea filled from the pure stream. The necessary fuel is speedily obtained from amongst the brushwood, and the guide is always provided with means to light it."

William Adam 'Gem of the Peak' 1851

Entrance to Renard's Hall, Dove Dale.

Eng. & Pub. by Newman & C. 48 Watling S. London.

"Pickering Tor, like Ilam Rock, has a neat cave in its base, and occupies a prominent position on the left of the path. The cave was formerly occupied by an aged recluse known locally as the Old Irish Woman who, through the generosity of visitors, local farmers and villagers, for many years eked out a precarious livelihood. When on her shopping excursions to Milldale or Alstonfield, she generally wore about all the clothing she possessed; therefore frequently presenting a most ludicrous and grotesque appearance. At times she was teased, but having a will of her own, youngsters as a rule, gave her a fairly wide berth. Her sleeping apartment was a smaller cave in the hillside, some distance up the adjoining gully. Eventually becoming rather menacing to visitors, she was removed to Leek, where she died in 1877."

The Golden Gorse Guide Through Dovedale

Eng.& Pub. by Newman & Cº 48 Watling St London.

Piccarry Tor. Dove Dale.

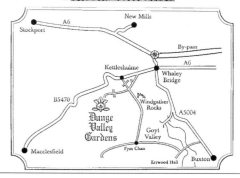

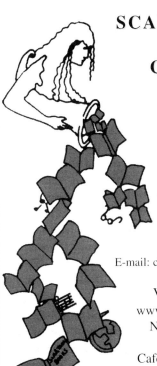

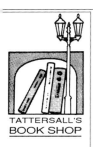

HAWKRIDGE BOOKS

Whether you are an avid reader or in search of a gift, we invite you to visit our bookshop to inspect our wide range of new, antiquarian and second hand books.

Ornithology and Natural History are our specialised subjects, but you will also find books on virtually any subject. For travelling book hunters, the Cruck Barn Cottage is situated in a quiet courtyard to the rear of the bookshop. Please ask for our brochure or contact Irene or Joe Tierney at:

HAWKRIDGE BOOKS

The Cruck Barn, Cross Street
Castleton, Sheffield S33 8WH
Tel. 01433 621999   Fax. 01433 621862
Open 10am to 5pm, seven days a week.
We are always interested in purchasing books in good condition.

THE IDEAL SETTING FOR YOUR FAMILY HOLIDAY

Just picture the setting – 44 acres of tranquil wooded area at the heart of the beautiful Derbyshire Peak District. Darwin Forest Country Park is ideally located for easy access to the splendour of the Peak District National Park, with many other attractions within easy reach.

So much to offer:-

- A choice of luxury "Pinelodge" self catering lodges with one, two, three or four bedrooms to accommodate up to eight adults.

- Superb indoor heated swimming pool.

- Foresters Inn serving an extensive menu in a traditional atmosphere.

- Tennis courts, mini-golf, adventure playground, games room and soft play area.

Darwin Forest Country Park, Darley Moor, Two Dales,
Matlock, Derbyshire DE4 5LN

PHONE **01629 732428**

FOR YOUR FREE BROCHURE

ACKNOWLEDGMENTS

*The publishers are grateful to Basil Jeuda and George Longden
for the loan of contemporary guide books
from which the quotations are taken.*

*Cover design and typesetting by
Christine Pemberton.*

*Printed by Redwood Books
Trowbridge, Wiltshire BA14 8RN*